WOM

ARTISTS

ce

GRAPHIC GUIDES
Series editor: Philip Boys

Apartheid
Donald Woods & Mike Bostock

Thatcher
Ed Harriman & John Freeman

Space Wars
Martin Ince & David Hine

Women Artists
Frances Borzello & Natacha Ledwidge

Forthcoming titles

Broadcasting
Peter Lewis & Corinne Pearlman

Language
Rob Pope & Graham Higgins

WOMEN ARTISTS

A GRAPHIC GUIDE

Frances Borzello and
Natacha Ledwidge

Camden Press

Published in 1986 by
Camden Press Ltd
43 Camden Passage, London N1 8EB, England

Text © Frances Borzello
Illustrations © Natacha Ledwidge
Designed by Sue Lacey

Set in 12 on 14pt Goudy Old Style
by Windhorse Photosetters
247 Globe Road, Bethnal Green, London E2
and printed and bound in Great Britain
by A Wheaton & Co, Exeter

British Library CIP Data
Frances Borzello
Women Artists: a graphic guide. – – –
(Graphic Guides)
1. Women artists.   2. Art – – – History
I. Title.   II. Ledwidge, Natacha
III. Series
709'.2'2   N8354

ISBN 0-948491-05-1 (pb)

PART ONE
YESTERDAY

Everyone knows what an artist looks like...

...a man with a velvet bow tie,
a smock, paint-spattered trousers,
a palette and –
indispensable accessory –

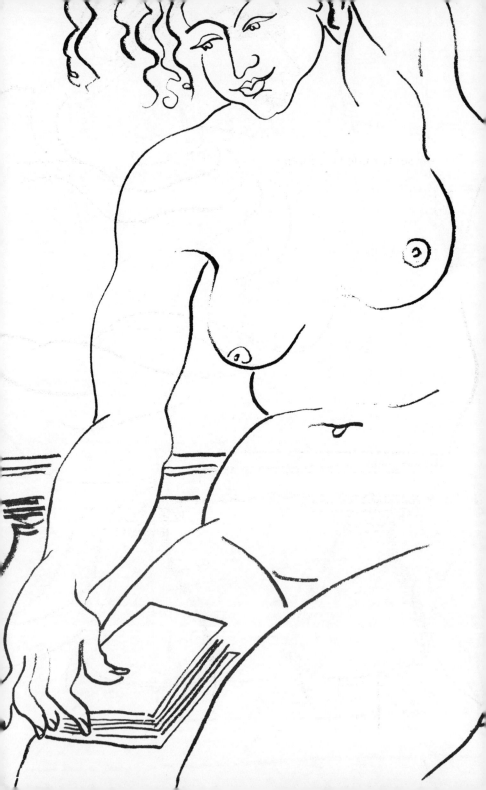

– a sexy, nude lady model.

But artists also looked like this:

Artemisia Gentileschi worked in the first half of the
seventeenth century in Italy and painted this self-portrait
to prove it.

There have always been women artists. Thousands of them. Whatever period of history you look at women can be found painting pictures, modelling clay or chipping away at stone, often in the most surprising places. In the fourteenth century Sabina von Steinbach carved these words on a scroll held by a sculpture of St John on the south portal of Strasbourg Cathedral: 'Thanks to the holy piety of this woman, Sabina, who from this hard stone gave me form.'

L. KNIGHT

DISMORR

SAMPERI

However unfriendly the social or intellectual climate, women have produced art – not just the embroidery, the quilts, the clothes and the textile designs that have traditionally been seen as the proper areas for women to work in – but fine art, Art with a capital A, the sort of art which gets put on to gallery walls and sold for high prices in sale rooms.

Women were hard at work in medieval times. It was not only the monasteries which produced illuminated and illustrated manuscripts as everyone is taught at school. There were illuminators in the nunneries – not so surprising when you consider their role as places where the intelligent, the intellectual, the talented woman could live in a society uncomplicated by male expectations of women. Cut off though they were from the pleasures of love and family life, they earned in return status, protection and the chance to develop their talents.

The greatest art produced by the English nunneries was the magnificent *opus Anglicanum*, the rich embroidery for ritual clothing famous throughout medieval Europe.

But signatures and illustrations in manuscripts produced in the nunneries and the secular scriptoria which developed in the thirteenth century show that women illustrators and illuminators were hard at work. In one, a nun hangs from the tail of an elaborate initialled letter. It must have been an aberration, since all the world knows women have no sense of humour!

Illuminate me
oh Lord...

Move on two hundred years to Renaissance Italy, normally thought of in terms of male artists like Leonardo, Botticelli, Raphael and Michelangelo, and there they are again, painting altarpieces (Lavinia Fontana), portraits (Sofonisba Anguissola), and great Biblical scenes on refectory walls (Plautilla Nelli). A little later, Artemisia Gentileschi depicted the deeds of brave women.

In seventeenth century Holland, Rachel Ruysch painted some of the most beautiful of the flower pieces that are the glory of Dutch art. Sybilla Merian produced prized botanical and butterfly illustrations for an age that was fascinated by the subject. Judith Leyster sued Franz Hals for stealing away one of her pupils.

In eighteenth century France a cluster of women painted alongside the men. Fragonard's sister-in-law Marguérite Gerard painted domestic genre scenes. Elizabeth Vigée-Lebrun painted royalty. Adélaïde Labille-Guiard specialized in training women to be painters. In Italy Rosalba Carriera convinced the fashionable that pastel portraits were high art.

From mid-nineteenth-century America a number of women sculptors went to Rome to practise their art, among them the single-minded Harriet Hosmer. She had a positive attitude to insults, which she called ' a bitter pill which we must all swallow at the beginning; but I regard these pills as quite essential to one's mental salvation.' Marriage she considered a 'moral wrong' for a woman artist, 'for she must neglect her profession or her family, becoming neither a good wife and mother nor a good artist.'

In late nineteenth century England a huge number of women artists emerged; some of them, like Louisa Jopling, Henrietta Rae and Elizabeth Thompson (later Lady Butler), becoming household names who drew crowds to their pictures at the Academy exhibitions. In France Rosa

Bonheur painted animals so successfully she became the first woman to be awarded the *Legion d'Honneur*, while Eva Gonzalez and Berthe Morisot proved that Impressionism was not an exclusively male preserve. At the turn of the century, the American Mary Cassatt dazzled Degas with her prints and paintings, becoming the figurehead for all the foreign women who went to Paris to learn to be great artists.

In the twentieth century, women have been linked to every movement and development in the art world. Paula Modersohn-Becker and Post-Impressionism in Germany. Sonia Terk Delaunay and Orphism in France. Natalia Goncharova and Rayonism in Russia. In every century, for every woman named there are hundreds standing behind and around her.

Berthe Morisot, Käthe Kollwitz, Mary Cassatt, Angelika Kauffmann, Bridget Riley, Barbara Hepworth, Georgia O'Keeffe, Rosa Bonheur, Artemisia Gentileschi... Artemisia who?

And that is the problem. Women artists exist, but they are hardly household names. It is easy to list ten male artists in ten seconds; it is much harder to list ten female artists.

Although naming the names of women painters is important it does not answer all the awkward questions. Why are there so few? Why have so few of their paintings survived? Why, if women painters have always existed, is it necessary to write books to prove it? Why, of the 800 artists represented in London's National Gallery, are only seven women?

For hundreds of years, the fact that there were fewer women artists than men was 'explained' in one of three ways.

'Explanation' No. 1 said that women lacked 'genius'.

The model for what is meant by genius is seen in Vasari's sixteenth century biographies of the artists. A typical example describes how Giotto, a young and untutored shepherd boy, was discovered by the artist Cimabue drawing on a stone as he watched his flocks.

According to this view, genius is something that will always out. It is a comforting belief, but in the case of young women with talent Gray's 'full many a flower is born to blush unseen and waste its sweetness on the desert air,' is more applicable.

The Giotto story pops up again and again down the ages; only the artists' names are changed. The implications for women are obvious. If there are no great women artists, it is because they lack talent. The weakness of this theory is that it ignores society's attitudes to women.

Were Cimabue to have found a shepherdess painting on a stone, he would probably have recognised her talent, shown her off as a freak – like an elephant balancing on a ball – and then seduced her.

'Explanation' No. 2 said that artists must be willing to suffer to get to the top.

Women, it's argued, did not have the drive; men, it goes without saying, did. Vincent van Gogh is the classic example of the truly committed artist. Kind, poor, un-appreciated, finally mad, he carried on painting through every setback, thereby winning an elevated position in the artistic fraternity.

But given that women were all too often told by society it was wrong to push or put themselves forward – from the beginning of recorded history men seem to have preferred their females compliant – it was unlikely that many would develop the confidence to do something that no women round them did, namely paint for a living. And to talk as if all who succeeded as artists did so because of their *drive* is unfair.

Van Gogh himself explodes that myth. That he was driven to paint is undeniable. Struggling genius he undoubtedly was. But struggling genius supported all his life by his brother Theo, who sent him money, found him doctors when he was sick, and above all listened sympathetically to the torrents of words he poured out in his letters.

The struggling genius explanation is cruel to women. Lack of money and opportunity, and the demands of father, husband and children, should make no difference to the flowering of genius, runs the argument. Any woman who wants to be an artist but allows herself to be daunted by such handicaps has therefore proved she is no artist.

'Explanation' No. 3 said that women's creative power went into rearing their children.

This male myth is as strong today as it was 400 years ago. As any woman knows, it is not creativity that gets used up in rearing children, it is *energy*. It is all too likely that a mother of small children would be too exhausted to paint after (let alone during) a day of caring for a family, but then so would a father. There is no proof that creative power is the possession of one sex more than the other. What we do know is that the opportunity to *express* that power certainly is.

These 'explanations' for the weak showing by women artists are unsatisfactory because they treat notions of *genius, talent, drive,* and *creativity* as if they have nothing to do with the conditions and circumstances of day-to-day life. They resemble the old-fashioned reasons for claiming that women did not make great chefs because they lacked 'flair' or 'temperament', when it was actually because they had never been allowed to train in the kitchens of the great restaurants. They have been used to prove that women possess no genius, or a different, inferior, genius from men.

And they have blocked the asking of the kinds of question that might have thrown light on the discrepancy between the numbers and greatness of male and female artists.

One of the earliest hard looks at why women failed professionally and still one of the most powerful is Virginia Woolf's *A Room of One's Own*. Published in 1928, it is a first person account of how she arrived at the conclusion that a woman must have money and a room of her own if she is to write fiction. Notice that there is no mention of genius.

She sets out to explain why there had been so few women writers, but the answers she comes up with and the evidence she uncovers apply equally to women artists. With wit and passion she lists the psychological as well as the practical barriers that discourage women from creative production.

Her greatest contribution to explaining women's meagre contribution to the arts is her analysis of the different male and female experience of life. She notes that while men of genius have faced indifference, women faced hostility. 'The world did not say to her, as it said to him, write if you choose; it makes no difference to me. The world said with a guffaw, "Write? What's the good of your writing?"' And she suggests that the psychologists of Cambridge colleges measure the effect of *discouragement* upon the mind of the artist.

She was not exaggerating. When asked his opinion on feminism in 1888, the painter Renoir wrote:

'I consider that women are monsters who are authors, lawyers and politicians, like George Sand, Madame Adam and other bores who are nothing more than 5-legged beasts. The woman who is an artist is merely ridiculous, but I feel that it is acceptable for a woman to be a singer or dancer.'

In 1971 Linda Nochlin asked, in an essay of the same name, why have there been no great women artists? The reason, she said, was that women had been denied an education as artists. Barred from the art schools, they had little hope of learning the skills which would equip them to compete with the men who dominated the field. This answer pulled the rug out from under the feet of believers in women's innate inability to produce art.

These two new approaches, the psychological and the

material, got the subject out of the mire of speculation and prejudice and onto the hard ground of history. Nearly all subsequent writing about women artists has built on them. Examinations of the social pressures on women *not* to succeed and of the lack of a sympathetic structure in which they could operate are the tools which researchers use to explain why so few works by women artists hang in galleries or turn up in dictionaries of paintings. The books and the articles produced in the last fifteen years show that women who aspired to make art have been systematically handicapped.

HANDICAPS

Handicap No. 1: Exclusion from the Academies

For hundreds of years the way to become an artist was to go to work in an artist's studio at the onset of adolescence, learning the trade from the bottom up. From the sixteenth century, another way existed – to study in an academy. There, students were told that the most important paintings – history paintings – were those with serious subject matter taken from the Bible and classical myths and they were taught the skills for producing them.

Both ways of learning were closed to women. This meant that women who held on to their ambition, talent and determination to paint were excluded by their lack of training from competing at the top level. For example, if you could not go to art school, you could not learn to draw from life. And if you could not learn to draw from life in the manner which the authorities agreed was correct you had no hope of producing paintings to the required standard. The history paintings which were the pinnacle of artistic accomplishment were beyond the reach of women because they had never learned to draw the nude body. When an ambitious woman artist arranged private tuition in order to compete with the men who set the standards, she was criticised.

In 1769, Angelika Kauffmann exhibited some of her mythological and classical subjects at the first exhibition of the newly-founded Royal Academy. 'Her women are most womanly and she conveys with much art the proper relation between the sexes, the dependence of the weaker on the stronger, which appeals very much to her masculine critics,' wrote Count Bernsdorff. 'It must be owned however that a little of this feebleness characterises her male personages. They are shy creatures; some of them look like girls in men's clothes...'

They do indeed look feminine. But then so do the men painted by many male artists at this time.

ANGELIKA KAUFFMANN

The problem was that once people knew a woman had painted a work, they looked – and inevitably found – what they considered to be signs of a woman's hand and mind.

Denied training, women concentrated on the less prestigious areas of art. Aware that the rules of constructing an important history picture were kept from them, they used their talents in the less demanding areas like flower paintings or portraits. And yet they were often criticised for this. People would say that while women were good copyists, they were hopeless at the 'higher' branches of art. No one considered that they had not been taught the higher branches. And no one talked about the male flower painters and portraitists in this way: they were specialising, not copying.

A third effect of lack of access to training was that women gave up the dream of becoming artists and channelled their need to create into other areas. They embroidered. They knitted. They designed and made clothes for their families or altered the ones they already had. They made gardens, and bed covers so beautiful they now sit in museums and fetch vast sums at auction. In 1774, Mary Delany developed the lady-like craft of making flower pictures out of coloured papers into so fine an art that the British Museum put them on show two centuries later. No-one minded women working in these areas. They did not get in anyone's way, and besides the end products were useful or decorative. It was true 'woman's work'. Yet they were working with what amounted in some cases to genius.

Around the middle of the nineteenth century, art academies began to admit women. It was 1860 when the Royal Academy, Britain's most prestigious school for artists, let in a woman student – by mistake. All hopeful candidates for admission had to submit a drawing of a piece of the human anatomy and the choice was made on the drawing skill displayed. One of the successful candidates for 1860 was 'L.H.' Since it had never occurred to the examiners that a woman might apply they were astounded when L.H. materialised into Laura Herford. They accepted her, but once inside she discovered as did all the other women who were taken into academies at the time that there was still a barrier against becoming a fully-trained professional painter: the authorities forbade them to follow the same course as the men. All major academies at this time took the student from drawing from plaster casts to drawing from life, *but the female students were not allowed to draw from the nude male model.* In the name of modesty, delicacy and the protection of female feelings, these institutions withheld the skills the women had come to learn.

The women tried to arrange their own life classes. After a day's work at the Royal Academy schools, keen women students would study drawing from the nude model at small private schools of art. Much is made of the 'true artist's' will to overcome all odds, but in fact the male students had a much easier time of it, working as they did in an institution which had been designed to teach them the alphabet of art. It was the women who had to struggle to become properly trained *within the institution itself.*

Finally, in 1893, the Royal Academy allowed the female students to draw from the male nude model. Or rather, nearly nude male model. His most precious and most private possession was hidden under nine feet of cloth wound tightly around his hips, securely held up with a belt. In the *Annual Report* for 1894, the rule was put into writing:

Annual Report

'The drapery to be worn by the model to consist of ordinary bathing drawers, and a cloth of light material 9 feet long by 3 feet wide, which shall be wound round the loins over the drawers, passed between the legs and tucked in over the waist-band, and finally a thin leather strap shall be fastened round the loins in order to insure that the cloth keeps its place.'

Handicap No. 2: Exclusion from Apprenticeships

It was possible for a lad from the lower classes to become an artist by learning a craft or skill and then graduating from that into fine art. For example, the eighteenth-century painter William Hogarth started life as a silver engraver.

This form of entry was closed to women, since workshops, guilds and apprenticeships were for men only. Only very rarely did a woman take this sort of path. Rosalba Carriera started with no advantages but ended up as the toast of the upper classes. Her pastel portraits of the rich and royal became a recognised type, so that successful women pastellists of the eighteenth century would be called the English or Italian or Danish Rosalba.

Her family was ordinary. Her father was a poorly paid government official and her mother a lace-maker (there was a painter grandfather for those who believe in heredity). The combination of her sex, class and the need to boost the family income while she was still in her teens, ensured that she set her sights low. Influenced by her mother, she started out designing lace. She progressed to snuffbox decoration, and then to miniature painting; finally learning anatomy in an artist's studio, a subject which she taught her sisters. (It is not at all clear how easy or how common it was for a young Venetian girl of the lower middle classes to learn anatomy, but until as much interest is taken in the pattern of female artists' careers as in that of men artists, we have no way of knowing.)

She remained unmarried and close to her family. Her sister Giovanna worked as her assistant, laying in the background and draperies and preparing the materials. She is commemorated in Rosalba's pastel self-portrait in which the artist holds a sketch of her sister. Assistants

must have been a problem for women artists: scandal
attached to the use of male assistants, but the pool of
trained women must have been tiny. All her journeys
abroad were made in the company of members of her
family; whether this was through choice or due to the
difficulty of a woman travelling alone, it is hard to know.

Handicap No. 3: The Wrong Sex for the Establishment

The women who benefited from the national art academies opening their doors had every confidence that they would succeed as artists. It was only after leaving that they found they were the wrong sex to succeed. For art is male. It is male in the sense that the law is male or nursing is female. The fact that there are lady lawyers or male nurses or even women artists only emphasises the domi-

nant gender of the profession. Whichever area of art you look at, the masculinity of art stares back at you.

The maleness of art directed how women were seen and how they acted in the art world. Women in the art world are models, muses, subject matter and the suppliers of supper and sex. They are ways for the male artist to prove what a full-blooded fellow he is.

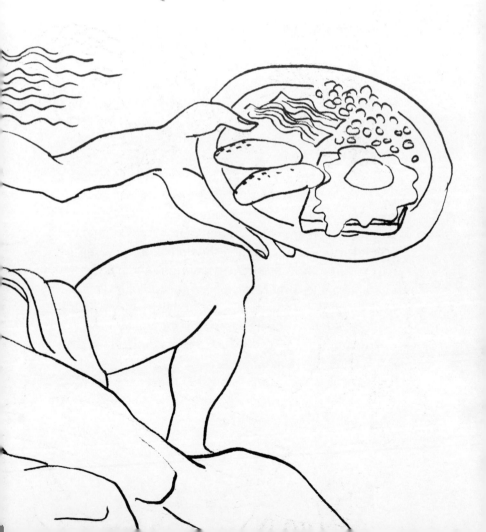

Men early on staked out art as their own territory. The artist has been a hero for a long time, fêted for his god-like ability to mirror the world and for his sexual prowess. This is as clear in the tales told by Pliny in the first century A.D. as in the tales of Picasso and his mistresses in recent times. In the Renaissance, with its stress on the individuality of artists as powerful in their way as royalty, there are many tales of kings bending down to pick up an artist's paintbrushes. In nineteenth century France with the development of the idea of Bohemia as a place where artistic licence meant licence with both art and women, the myth grew even stronger.

Beautiful or useful women were allowed into this world, but very few women artists. At the end of the nineteenth century Degas was friends with Mary Cassatt, taking her seriously as a painter, and he encouraged the model Suzanne Valadon to paint as well. Angelika Kauffmann was accepted as an equal by many eighteenth century artists.

But these are rare examples. More common was the male attitude that admired and loved women as long as they stayed on the far side of the easel. Renoir, a great painter of women, believed that men should be the thinkers and artists, while women should be sources of pleasure for men in sex, in mothering, and in homemaking. How uncomfortable it must have been for the painters Berthe Morisot and Eva Gonzales to know that one of their colleagues felt like that, or for Suzanne Valadon, who was producing her first works while she modelled for artists – Renoir among them.

Patronage and connoisseurship have always been a male affair because men have had the money and the education. There have been women patrons of the arts but like the women artists they have been lost among the men. For every painting of Mme de Pompadour surrounded by the books, the drawings and the music she encouraged, there are hundreds of paintings of male patrons. In Zoffany's paintings of *Charles Towneley's Library in Park Street* (1781-3), with its classical casts and its male connoisseurs, the only female intrusion into the rarefied air of scholarship are the nude sculptures.

In William Orpen's painting of the *New English Art Club* (1918), all the faces with the power to select works for the forthcoming exhibition are male.

Men controlled the groups and clubs and made sure women didn't enter. Without the possibility of belonging to groups, women artists were isolated in their work. They didn't have the support system enjoyed by many male artists and they were unable to infiltrate the artistic network in the way a group with a manifesto could.

In her study of the Camden Town Group, Wendy Baron reports that Sickert attributed the evolution of the group's method of painting 'with a clean and solid mosaic of thick paint in a light key' to the combined efforts of artists belonging to the New English Art Club, 'for these things are done in gangs, not by individuals.'

It was a gang which did not go out of its way to welcome women. Said Sickert:

'As a matter of fact, the Camden Town Group is a male club, and women are not eligible. There are lots of two sex clubs, and several one sex clubs, and this is one of them.'

All the most important artistic institutions were run by men. The Royal Academy had forty founding members – 38 men and 2 women, Mary Moser and Angelika Kauffmann. But it's clear they weren't really members of the club. In Zoffany's portrait the founding fathers are pictured in the life class surrounding two male models while the founding mothers are depicted as paintings on the walls. It was historically accurate since the life class was forbidden to ladies, but Zoffany may also have thought he was paying a compliment to the women by suggesting that they were as pretty as pictures. But to modern eyes it looks as if he has depicted them in their traditional role as the objects, not the creators, of art.

Many academies of art awarded honorary medals and memberships, and several women won them. But they were not all that much use. True power came from being a full member of these bodies, with the right to vote and voice opinions. Here the academies were not so keen.

The bar against women becoming Academy members had nothing to do with their lack of talent and everything to do with the fact that fine art at a professional level was a man's world. In 1874 Elizabeth Thompson painted *Roll Call*, which made such a stir at the Royal Academy that Queen Victoria asked to be shown it.

This was followed by two more military scenes, *Quatre Bras* in 1875 and *Balaclava* in 1876, which were so successful that the Academy voted to decide whether the artist should be made a member. The vote went against her. Explains the official historian of the Royal Academy:

'Despite the inclusion of Angelika Kauffmann and Mary Moser in the original foundation, the Council made the rather surprising announcement that, in their opinion, by the letter of the law, the Instrument did not provide for the election of females.

In specifying eligibility for membership, it uses the phrase "men of fair moral character", and, in their opinion, this had to be interpreted as not including women.'

As always, men define the meaning of 'men'. When women complain that 'men' excludes them, the men say that everyone knows that 'men' means mankind and includes both sexes. When men want to exclude women, they say 'men' means the male sex.

After turning Elizabeth Thompson down, the official biographer says that 'they framed a resolution to make women eligible but limited their "privileges". The matter then seems to have been forgotten, as no women were elected till Annie Swynnerton and Laura Knight in the 1920s.'

Women were allowed to operate on the fringes of the art world but they were denied access to the professional structure, which was the only way they would be taken seriously and could make their views felt. Women were so used to this, they pretended they did not mind. In *An Autobiography*, published in 1922, Elizabeth Thompson, by then Lady Butler, recalled:

'I think the difficulties of electing a woman were great, and much discussion must have been the consequence amongst the R.A.s. However, as it turned out, in 1879, I lost my election by *two* votes only! Since then I think the door has been closed, and wisely.'

The tradition of art being male was so strong that there was little chance for a female tradition to thrive. Because all the most famous artists were men, the women artists naturally measured themselves against them. To start a female tradition, calling up precursors and collaborating with other women artists in groups and exhibitions, must have seemed an unwise strategy to women who had reached a successful position in the art world. Would Berthe Morisot or Angelika Kauffmann or Elizabeth Thompson ally themselves to a sex that the majority of male artists in their circle considered incapable of painting a decent picture?

Handicap No.4: Society's View of Femininity

It was not merely a feeling that women should not put themselves forward. It was also that society with the aid of religion, culture and morality had constructed a way of arranging the roles which both sexes accepted as common sense. Women have always known that though they had to conform to these gender roles they were not always in their interests. In 1869, Berthe Morisot wrote to her sister who had given up painting on her marriage and was living a life she described as 'the fireside, and the rain pouring down'.

...Men incline to believe that they fill all of one's life, but as for me, I think that no matter how much affection a woman has for her husband, it is not easy for her to break with a life of work.

Nonetheless, if everyone around you believed that it was unfeminine to put your demands for education or for the right to an easel and paint before those of your husband, your parents or your children, you would have to be unusually self-confident to fight to be anything but the least troublesome sort of artist. Your friends and family would welcome your portraits and local landscapes. But if you started to Get Ideas, demanding a studio and the right to paint through meal times, your welcome skill would rapidly turn into a nuisance.

Dora Carrington was an English artist who with encouragement would have developed into a respectable talent. At the Slade School of Art her work was praised but, after leaving, like many women she gave more time to relationships than to her painting. Her inability to prevent her personal life from interrupting her work is a blueprint for the thousands of talented women who failed to live up to their promise. Asked by Virginia Woolf to illustrate a book, she turned down the commission on the grounds that her great love, the writer Lytton Strachey, was ill.

... But to come to business. How can I do wood blocks when for the last month, ever since in fact we left Northumberland, I've been a ministering angel, hewer of wood and drawer of water?

When the art critic Clive Bell came to stay, she wrote:

Clive Bell and Mrs Hutchinson came here last weekend. They aren't my style. Too elegant and eighteenth century French for that's what they try to be. I felt my solidity made them dislike me. Then I had to make their beds, and empty chamber pots because our poor cook Mrs. Legg can't do everything and that made me hate them, because in order that they should talk so elegantly, I couldn't for a whole weekend do any painting and yet they scorned my useful grimy hands!

It is useless to get irritated with her or demand that she pull herself together. The social roles set down for men and women made it almost automatic for her to give up the art and devote herself to domesticity. What she needed was what Lytton had: a devoted companion who could encourage her and simplify her life so she could be free to paint. As it is, she goes down in history as an unstretched painter, a fringe member of Bloomsbury and a woman who could not live without her love. Six weeks after Strachey died of cancer, Carrington committed suicide.

Role rules were so widespread that they affected the women's self confidence. Virginia Woolf wrote in *A Room of One's Own*:

'Let us suppose that a father from the highest motives did not wish his daughter to leave home and become a writer, painter or school teacher. "See what Mr Oscar Browning says," he would say; and there was not only Mr Oscar Browning; there was the *Saturday Review*; there was Mr Greg – "the essentials of a woman's being," said Mr Greg emphatically, "are that they are supported by, and they minister to, men" – there was an enormous body of masculine opinion to the effect that nothing could be expected of women intellectually. Even if her father did not read out loud these opinions, any girl could read them for herself; and the reading, even in the nineteenth century, must have lowered her vitality, and told profoundly upon her work.'

Widely accepted prejudices about women's place even affected the women who were let into the art schools. The painter Hubert Herkomer opened a school of painting for both sexes in England in 1883 and his autobiography, *My School and My Gospel*, abounds with examples of the sort of lowering opinions referred to by Virginia Woolf.

'It is strange that the majority of women students are untidy workers. In going round their class, it needed some careful piloting not to run against overfilled brushes, or stumble over paintboxes and odd brushes on the floor. I would not even like to vouch for their faces. But on this subject, I must say no more, or I may get into trouble.

'Now it happened that there were students, especially amongst the women, who thought they knew better than I did as to the proper methods of painting, and aired their views freely to the class in my absence.'

His evidence came from a student's diary:

My Diary

There was a new girl in the liferoom who gave us her views about painting the flesh. She declared, very authoritatively, that it could never be done satisfactorily without under-painting in some complementary colour, and added that all this painting 'alla prima' was nonsense... Well, she proceeded to paint the whole torso with Indian red and white... Suddenly, on the Friday morning, the Professor appeared... he looked long at the study, then turned to look at her, then back to the study, then without uttering a word, or showing a sign of what he thought, he turned away to examine another student's work!

When a female student married, she was no longer eligible for the school.

'The women were in great fear that I should turn them out of the school when they became engaged, and they tried hard to keep the matter secret from me.

'From the start I refused to take married women. A lady came with her husband who seemed in the depths of misery at the idea of his wife studying in the "life". The statement that married women were ineligible for my school had scarcely passed

my lips when his entire expression changed, and he beamed with delight. The wife's last appeal was: "But I am so fond of drawing; what am I to do if I cannot study?" That was easily answered: "Devote your life to the happiness of your husband and children." The husband lingered a little after his angry wife had passed out of my drawing-room, and pressed my hand with great warmth, saying:

'I remember another married lady coming to see me. She had left her mother in an open carriage at the gate. The younger lady, who received the same answer as the others, very pathetically urged that she was a widow, and she could not quite see the point that a woman, once married, was always married. The mother, a tall, largely-built masculine sort of woman, heard the result of the interview with evident indignation. "What right have you to deny my daughter entrance to your school simply because she has been married? She has to work for her children, and painting is the only thing she is fit for." I was far too amused to be angry; but I confess I got a little anxious when the old lady's face, which on entering my drawing-room was of an ashy paleness, began to get redder and redder. Hence my palliative answer. "Madam, it is very complimentary to me that you should be so anxious for your daughter to study art in my school, but my law in respect to married women is irrevocable." She returned to the attack: "Why can't you alter it? It is a monstrous law, and I cannot congratulate you on it." And out she stalked, her back rigid, her head jerking from side to side.'

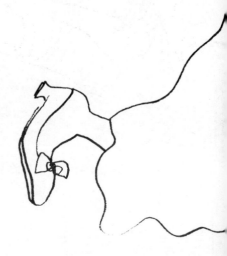

Hubert Herkomer's school was one of the few 'opportunities' offered to would-be women painters at the end of the nineteenth century. It is hard to believe that the teaching they got there was unaffected by his prejudices. Ironically, it was a female student, Lucy Kemp Welch, who brought his school its greatest honour when one of her paintings was purchased for the Royal Academy.

A particularly deadly effect of the acceptance of gender roles was that male chivalry towards women made them overload with praise work that in no way deserved it. John Ruskin, the English writer whose views on art overshadowed most of the second half of the nineteenth century, was forever praising favoured women painters, like the illustrator Kate Greenaway, in the most lavish terms, while at the same time believing them incapable, because of their sex, of producing Great Art. If he, and so many like him, had given the women some useful criticism and practical advice, their art might have lived up to his eulogies.

Gender roles led men to believe they knew better and women to believe they should accept the prescription. Berthe Morisot describes the time her future brother-in-law, the artist Edouard Manet, came to help her out with a painting:

'The next day, which was yesterday, he came at about one o'clock; he found it very good, except for the lower part of the dress. He took the brushes and put in a few accents that looked very well; mother was in ecstasies. That is where my misfortunes began. Once started, nothing could stop him; from the skirt he went to the bust, from the bust to the head, from the head to the background. He cracked a thousand jokes, laughed like a madman, handed me the palette, took it back; finally by five o'clock in the afternoon we had made the prettiest caricature that was ever seen. The carter was waiting to take it away; he made me put it on the hand-cart, willy-nilly. and now I am left confounded. My only hope is that I shall be rejected. My mother thinks this episode funny, but I find it agonising.'

Society's expectations of how women should behave set up conflicts in women artists that their male counterparts did not have to face. However successful they became, they constantly had to prove that they remained 'feminine'.

This conflict shows in their self-portraits. Though a number of them show women proudly at work, the majority show the artists as women first, painters second.

A male artist does not have to pass what amounts to a masculinity test when he does his own portrait. Any way he depicts himself is acceptable. In the eighteenth century you find Chardin in an eye shade, Hogarth sitting at his easel without his wig, Luis Menendez dressed to the nines and displaying his drawing of a nude male model. In all these portraits the men stress the working aspect of their profession with great pride but display little personal vanity. In some cases they use the absence of vanity about their appearance to underline their seriousness as artists.

But there was no way women could build on such proto-
types. An eighteenth-century audience – one which
invented the term bluestocking as a term of mockery of
intellectual women – would have laughed at a woman
painter in eyeglasses. Nor could the eighteenth century
have stomached a lady painter holding a drawing of a nude
male model. For one thing it would have lacked credibil-
ity, and for another the gossip aroused by such subject
matter would have ruined her reputation.

When the eighteenth century's female artists produce self-portraits, their palettes and brushes have the air of attractive accessories. The successful Elizabeth Vigée-Lebrun often presented herself with an arm round her daughter, showing that good though she was at her profession, she was a mother at heart and therefore no threat to the men.

Part of the problem was that there was no pattern for female artists' self portraits. Women in portraits were rarely shown doing anything and were always painted to look as pretty as possible. Adélaïde Labille-Guiard cleverly uses this convention to stress her success as an artist. Clad in an impossibly impractical satin gown and a hat so large it must hinder her vision, she sits proudly at her easel, her two pupils – for she had a studio – leaning on the back of her chair like two maids of honour attending a bride. Her finery, which is that of an imposing matron rather than a coquette, in combination with the emphatic position of her palette and easel, makes her a woman to be reckoned with.

It was over 100 years before Laura Knight's self-portrait (1913) equalled Labille-Guiard's air of professional competence and confidence.

Handicap No. 5: Sexual Innuendo

Sexual innuendo has always attached itself to women artists like pins to a magnet. An aura of sex clings to male artists as well, but it works to their advantage. There is a tradition of tales of male artists with heroic sexual appetites from Raphael in the sixteenth century to Picasso in the twentieth. They paint their mistress as the Virgin Mary and run away with novice nuns (Fra. Filippo Lippi). They get through mistresses as fast as art materials (Augustus John) while Morality obligingly smiles on.

But in art, as in everything, a double standard prevails. When sex is linked to women artists, it is never to their advantage. Although art schools kept women from studying the nude male model until the end of the nineteenth century, a determined woman could make her own arrangements to do so. If, that is, she was prepared to endanger her reputation.

The rumours that Angelika Kauffmann drew from the male nude model when she was working in London in the 1760s and 1770s outlived her death in 1807. Twenty years later the sculptor Nollekens's biographer, John Thomas Smith, determined to find out if there was any truth to them:

'It having been asserted that Angelika Kauffmann studied from an exposed male living model, which Mr. Nollekens said he believed, I was determined to gain the best information on the subject by going to Mr. Charles Cranmer, one of the original models of the Royal Academy, now living, in his eighty-second year, at No.13, in Regent Street, Vauxhall Bridge; and he assured me that he did frequently sit before Angelika Kauffmann at her house on the south side of Golden Square, but that he only exposed his arms, shoulders and legs, and that her father, who was also an artist and likewise an exhibitor at the Royal Academy, was always present.'

74

As a prominent woman artist, Angelika was fair game for the gossips of the day. In 1775 the Irish artist Nathaniel Hone painted a satirical picture aimed at Sir Joshua Reynolds, president of the Royal Academy. Reports Smith:

'There was at first some indelicacy which he had introduced in the centre of the picture, but which he afterwards painted out, respecting a slanderous report which had been whispered as to Sir Joshua and Angelika Kauffmann.'

Smith is appalled but fascinated by the wicked Angelika. Commenting on her unfortunate marriage to a bogus Swedish count, Smith says that Angelika 'was universally considered as a coquette, so that we cannot deeply sympathize in her disappointment.' As evidence of how justly she deserved the label of coquette, he reports that at Rome before her marriage she stood between two admirers at the theatre,

'and finding an arm of each most lovingly embracing her waist, she contrived, whilst her arms were folded before her on the front of the box over which she was leaning, to squeeze the hand of both, so that each lover concluded himself beyond all doubt the man of her choice.'

A high profile can help the artist to an elevated status...

Handicap No. 6: Exclusion from Artistic Life

Becoming a successful artist involves more than showing in exhibitions, catching the critics' eye and selling work, important though these are. It helps to be a 'personality'. It is not necessary to have a high profile to be taken seriously, but it can help to elevate an artist's status. Carrington had no one to sing her praises. Her friends did not talk about her as an artist, and she rarely talks about herself as one.

By contrast, Augustus John, painting at the same time, *was* a personality. He travelled in a gypsy caravan. He had several lovely children by several lovely women. He was so lecherous that Carrington joked about travelling in a taxi with him and *not* having a pass made at her. He taught for a time, which meant he influenced a lot of young painters. He became a Royal Academician. He painted the portraits of the beautiful, the rich and the great. And he figures in everyone's memoirs. A high public profile can tip the balance between recognition and lack of it. Which brings us to...

Handicap No. 7: Victimisation by Art History

Art history is written by art historians who, being human, will write more about artists they know lots about. Augustus John is a case in point. Famous though he was, the critics and connoisseurs never considered him a top-notch painter. Yet for all their doubts he appears in the histories of art. In the Pelican History of Art volume, *Painting and Sculpture in Europe 1880-1914*, George Heard Hamilton writes:

'John (1878-1961) dazzled his contemporaries for half a century and more by his singular facility as a draughtsman and portrait-ist, although he brought to the latter little that was new in the way of psychological understanding or even of design, and his drawings all too often betray his dependence on the masters of the past.'

It may be lukewarm, but it is there, and with an illustra-tion as well. But Augustus's sister Gwen John, whom many consider a better artist than her brother, is nowhere mentioned. What this means is that if you go to this reputable reference book for enlightenment, you come away knowing that Augustus John was an artist – albeit a not particularly good one – but with no inkling that he had a sister who was better. If Augustus John is such a mediocre painter why discuss him at all? It can only be a reflection of his outsize personality and the role he played in the artistic life of England.

Nonetheless despite the obstacles, many women became professional artists. Some of them even became famous. How did they manage it?

ADVANTAGES

Advantage No. 1: An Artist for a Father

A great advantage – almost a necessity – for a woman who wanted to paint seriously enough to compete with the men who set the standards was to have an artist father. This was particularly useful in the centuries when women were denied access to training in workshops or academies. If father was an artist – as Artemisia Gentileschi's was – she could learn the complete craft of painting, from grinding the pigment to preparing the wood panel or canvas for the paint. The disadvantage was that she risked becoming an unpaid, unpraised assistant in the workshop, painting the parts of the portraits, like the acres of skirt or background, that are never noticed, leaving the hands and the faces to the master. Although a large number of women profited from their family background to propel themselves into an artistic career, there were a great many more who remained shadows in their fathers' studios.

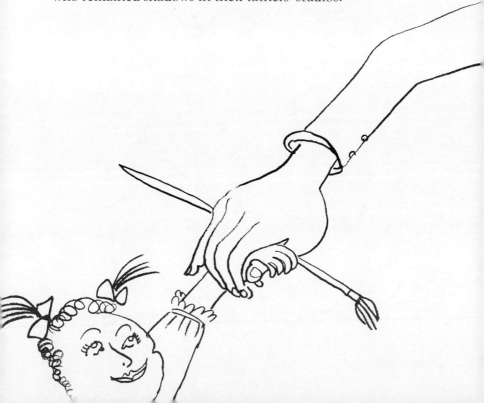

Advantage No. 2: A Rich Family

Sofonisba Anguissola was fortunate in having a father who believed in educating not only his son but his six daughters as well. Though not unusual for daughters of rich and enlightened families to be taught to paint and draw by good masters, it was unusual for them to take the leap into professionalism. No matter how skilful, their status as gentlewomen forbad them to compete in the market place. Lack of need for a career, plus notions of what was suitable behaviour and occupation for women, meant that such education rarely developed beyond the pretty talent stage. The first teacher of the Morisot sisters warned their parents to be cautious.

Sofonisba Anguissola made the leap into professionalism. She was invited – and went – to the court of Philip II of Spain. The position of women artists at Renaissance courts is interesting and unresearched. It seems that royalty liked to have the occasional woman artist around, perhaps as a sort of prodigy, perhaps because she could be put safely to work teaching art to the female members of the royal family. It would be fascinating to know how common it was in the sixteenth century for a woman to travel to Spain. Was an invitation from royalty enough to overcome the objections of family and society? Or were there no such objections for nobly-born women? Did it

help that she was unmarried for the twenty years she spent at the court?

In 1556, Queen Mary of Hungary, regent of the Netherlands, took Katharina de Hemessen and her husband, organist of Antwerp Cathedral, off to the court of her nephew, Philip II of Spain. It was obviously some sort of accolade, but at this distance and with so few facts it is impossible to know whether Katharina was seen as a super portraitist or whether Queen Mary liked the idea of introducing an arty double act of musician husband and painter wife to the Spanish court.

Advantage No. 3: Supportive Parents

Women artists have frequently given their fathers credit for encouraging their talent. After her mother's death, Angelika Kauffmann and her father travelled through Europe enabling Angelika to meet the influential and famous. She painted the portrait of the great art theorist Winckelmann in Rome, and in Venice in 1766 she met the British ambassador's wife, who brought her to England.

No doubt the father, who was not half so good an artist as his daughter, flaunted her talent to gain fame and fortune. But since the normal routes to recognition were closed to women, he had to operate outside the conventional system.

Rosa Bonheur's father, a weak painter but a strong believer in the rights of women, was perfectly willing to let his daughter keep a goat in their Paris apartment if it helped in the accuracy of her art.

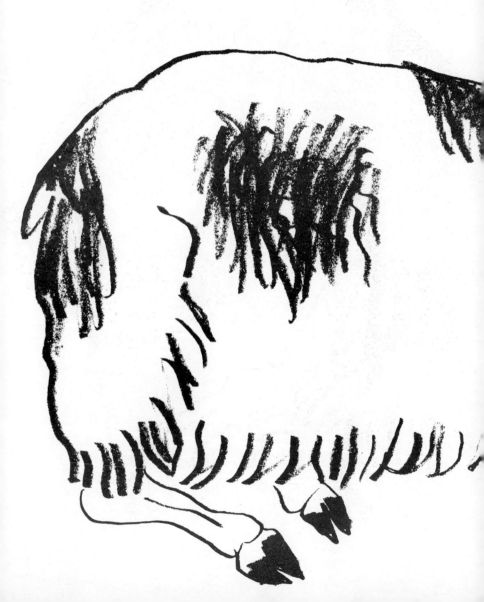

Mothers, denied education and social mobility, could offer little practical help in furthering a daughter's career but they gave psychological support. Berthe Morisot's mother encouraged her three daughters' desire to study art. In a letter to Berthe in 1867 she retails some gossip of an evening party, noting that 'There was less talk about your painting, it seemed to me, than about your person.' And she concludes: 'Men indeed have all the advantages and make life comfortable for themselves; I am not spiteful, but I hope there will be a compensation.' In 1871 Mme Morisot discussed with her daughter Edma her decision to support Berthe in her painting ambitions:

'I hope for only one thing now – that you are right and that Berthe can become independent. I for my part do not believe so at all, but I shall do everything I can to help her reach her goal; it is at least an objective – after all, one has to do something in life. But what an arduous task it is! Whenever she works she has an anxious, unhappy, almost fierce look. I cannot say how

much of this comes from wounded pride, but I do know that this existence of hers is like the ordeal of a convict in chains and I should like to enjoy greater peace of mind in my old age.'

Advantage No. 4: A Fashionable Style

Artemisia Gentileschi was impressed and inspired by the
painting of Caravaggio, an Italian artist whose realistic
and dramatic way of painting scenes from the Bible
revolutionised European art for the first four decades of the
seventeenth century.

She painted in the prevailing Caravaggiste fashion, using his manner of spotlighting gestures to make her subject matter come across more strongly to the viewer, but she was no copyist.

As an Impressionist in late nineteenth century France, Berthe Morisot worked in the most avant-garde manner of her day. Yet being part of an avant garde was not without its special dangers for a woman. When a critic referred to the second Impressionist Exhibition – at which Berthe showed 20 works – as 'organised by five or six lunatics, one of whom is a woman,' her husband challenged him to a duel. The article concluded:

'There is also a woman in the group, as is the case with all famous gangs. Her name is Berthe Morisot, and she is interesting to behold. In her, feminine grace is preserved amidst the frenzy of a mind in delirium.'

The critic's striving to make Berthe fit his stereotypes turns her into a sort of well-bred gangster's moll.

Elizabeth Thompson painted successfully for the late Victorian art public, which admired her large, action-packed pictures, the forerunners of the epic silent films which emerged at the start of the next century. By sticking to battle scenes, she found a formula that fitted into the prevailing fashion yet stood out above it.

Advantage No. 5: A Sympathetic Era

The women reigned them; the Revolution dethroned them,

wrote Elizabeth Vigée-Lebrun about eighteenth century France in her memoirs. It is no coincidence that the second half of the eighteenth century, with its admiration of refined behaviour and pretty, witty women, produced a number of successful women artists. They succeeded because their combination of looks and talent was welcome in an age whose upper class society was of an indoor and artificial kind. Elizabeth Vigée-Lebrun was merely the most famous of these artists; there were many others. Vigée-Lebrun became a painter to Queen Marie Antoinette while still in her twenties; after the revolution she was a welcome guest at royal courts in an assortment of European countries. As a woman, she played by the rules and trod on no toes; as a portrait painter she flattered the rich, famous and well born. In her autobiography she recalls how the first painter to the king opposed her election to the Royal Academy of Painting on the grounds that *women* should not be admitted, though as she pointed out, there were already two female members. As a painter to the Queen, she got her place, but this attempt at keeping a woman out of a male art club taught her the wisdom that charm and tact were as important a factor as talent in her success.

Advantage No. 6: Famous Clients

One way to stay visible is to paint important people. If you have painted a queen or a king your name will go down in history – on the bottom right hand corner of the portrait. It also helps to paint pictures that cannot be moved. Angelika Kauffmann decorated the walls and ceilings of a number of grand buildings and hence is built into art history.

Advantage No. 7: A Place in the Art World

Being a friend or a lover of an artist, or being a member – even a minor member – of an artistic group, can write a woman artist's name into the records.

Vanessa Bell, the sister of Virginia Woolf, painted all her life. As a founding member of the the Bloomsbury group she was involved in many of the adventures and theories of its associates. Through her relationship with Roger Fry she was in at the start of the abstract art movement in England. When he brought the works of French artists like Gauguin and Matisse to England for the second Post-Impressionist show in 1912, he included some of Bell's paintings, done in the new manner which played down subject matter and emphasized colours and shapes. Two years later she produced designs for the Omega Workshop, Fry's attempt at supporting artists by paying them a weekly wage in return for designing domestic items. Between the two world wars, she and Duncan Grant covered the interiors and furniture of the rich and arty with brightly coloured patterns.

For years people who had never seen her paintings – for they were rarely reproduced – knew that Vanessa Bell was an artist through the references to her in other people's biographies and autobiographies. Kept in the public eye through her connection with major figures and art movements, she is today herself the subject of biographies.

A similar principle applies to the women artists of the second half of the nineteenth century who joined in the fashion for artistic autobiographies. The kind of academic paintings they produced are out of favour today, but their lives exist in libraries.

Advantage No. 8: Self Confidence

It is hard to hang on to your self-confidence in a profession which prefers to see you as light relief, a small talent who smiles a lot. But some women managed it for reasons that can only be found in their psychology, their parents' support and sometimes in their failure to absorb the conditioning that made them 'real women' in society's eyes.

Educated by her father and by copying the paintings in the Louvre, Rosa Bonheur had her first picture in the Paris Salon when she was 19. Nine years later she was awarded the Salon's gold medal for *Ploughing in the Nivernais*, which the French Government bought for the Louvre. Four years later, in 1853, she painted one of the most famous animal paintings of the nineteenth century, the enormous *Horse Fair*, eight by sixteen and a half feet. It was exhibited in England for a sixpence entrance fee, shown to Queen

Victoria by royal request, and ended up as a print on
thousands of parlour walls.

Rosa Bonheur's way of coping with the social pressures
on women artists was to pretend to be a man. To avoid
being harassed at the horse fair, she got permission from
the Paris police to dress as a man – and she kept to that
dress for the next forty years. She kept practical problems
at bay by living with Natalie Micas and her mother for
many years, and then, on Natalie's death, taking up with
the young American painter Anna Klumpke.

In her decision to love and live as much like a man as
she could, she was following the pattern set up by her male
contemporaries, the nineteenth century academic artists
whose wives treated them like gods, and ensured that, like
gods, they had little to do with the mundane side of life.

Advantage No. 9: Single Mindedness

Just as Rosa Bonheur decided to be a man, Gwen John decided to cut herself off from the society that threatened to hinder her from giving herself full-time to her art. She could hardly have failed to notice that the women artists who came too close to her brother Augustus – like Ida Nettleship, his first wife, and Dorelia McNeill, his second – were never given the time or the encouragement to paint.

In her late twenties she settled in France. She was lonely, suffered from a mostly unrequited love for the sculptor Rodin, and fed the cats she adored better than she fed herself. Clearly eccentric, she was nevertheless clever enough to escape being sucked into the role of aunt in her famous brother's extended family, or to have her unconventional life-style hampered by well-meaning English friends.

PART TWO
TODAY

Half of the students on fine art courses in this country are female. But half of the professional artists in this country are not.

Fewer contemporary women artists than men

...teach in art schools
...have regular dealers
...are selected for survey shows
...have their work reviewed
...are awarded grants
...are chosen as artists-in-residence
...appear in gallery listings
...have one-person shows

So what happens to the women who start off at art school with the same hopes and enthusiasms as the men? Some drop out of college, or give up the idea of making a living from art soon after graduation, but not in such numbers as to explain the domination of the field by male artists. Some get married, but then so do the men and it doesn't stop them painting. Some have children, but male artists become fathers and continue to work.

The real reasons lie deeper.

The first reason is that society tells women that to be successful they must be single-minded, but it makes them feel unfeminine if they are. This double message stops women fighting. They know that 'unattractive' and 'aggressive' are the ways of describing a woman's ambition,

and they know that 'feminine' means putting others' needs first. Women have internalised centuries of guilt about doing their own thing before looking after everyone else's needs.

Put at its most basic, a woman in a family cannot settle down at the drawing board till she has cleaned the bath. No matter that it is silly to feel that way; no matter that husbands and children may not notice the state of the bath. Her conscience, social prejudices, fear of being a bad homemaker, the desire to please which seems built into so many women, will eat into her hours at the easel. An income from her art would justify her concentrating on her art. But paradoxically, before she can earn she needs to *spend* time perfecting her talent.

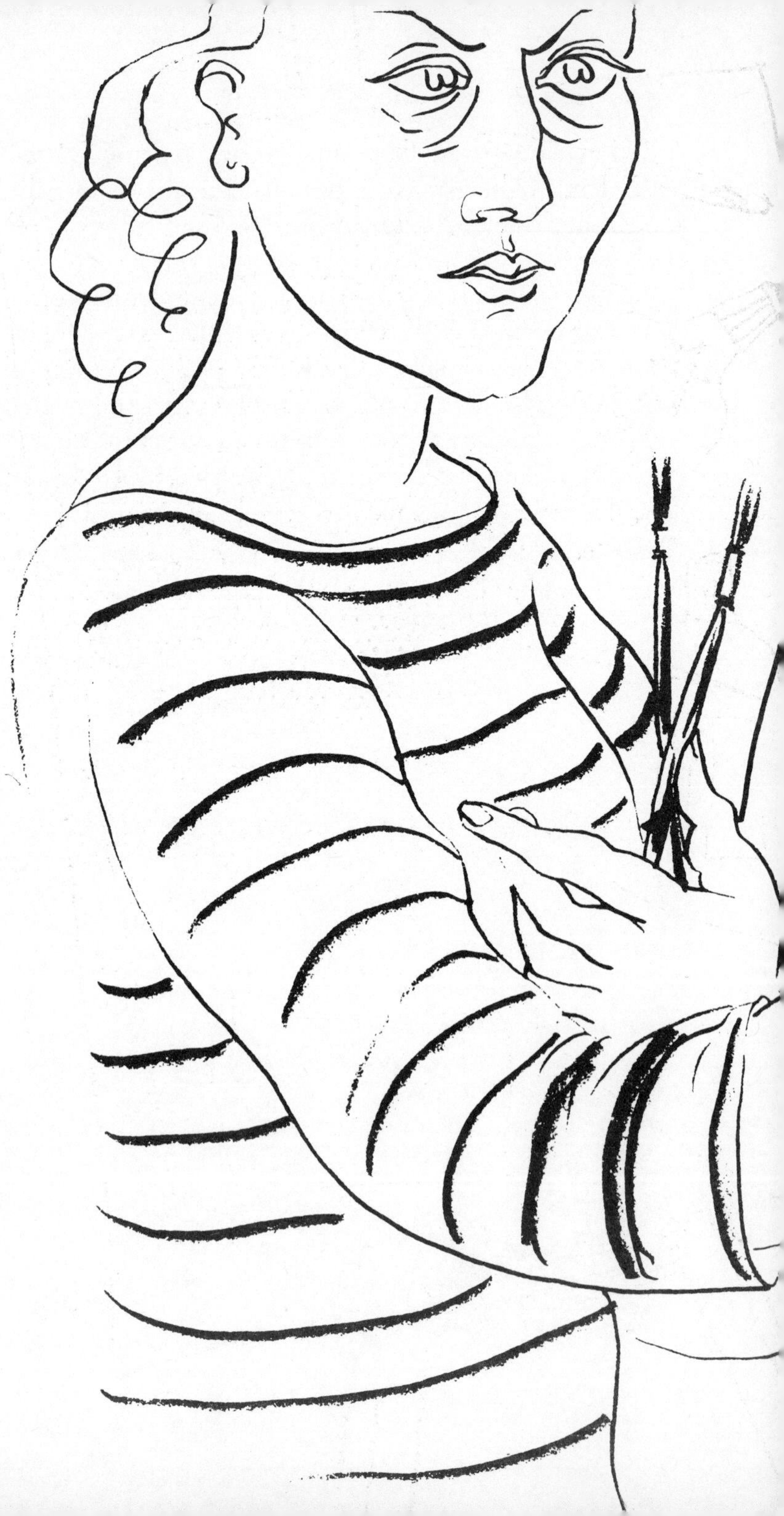

The second reason is that society has not decided how much opportunity it wants to give women. It pays lip service to equality, but in reality does not offer it. Though women are allowed to train to be professional artists, they find it hard to get work. Men too find it difficult, but when teaching jobs, competitions and curatorships are offered, more men get them than women. There is a lingering prejudice – even in an age of husbandless families, or families where two incomes are necessary to cover the running costs – that it is the man who is the breadwinner and that he is therefore entitled to the first crack at any job going.

The third is that art is still, as it always has been, male. Museums, galleries and art schools, whether private or public, are run by men, with predominantly male boards of trustees.

One of the mysteries of the art world is how this happens, since the courses which produce the experts are made up of equal numbers of male and female students. The class structure of art only allows the female second-class citizens into the less prestigious areas of teaching – in schools, colleges of further education and polytechnics, and in the applied and decorative art departments of the art schools.

NOT ANOTHER REDHEAD!

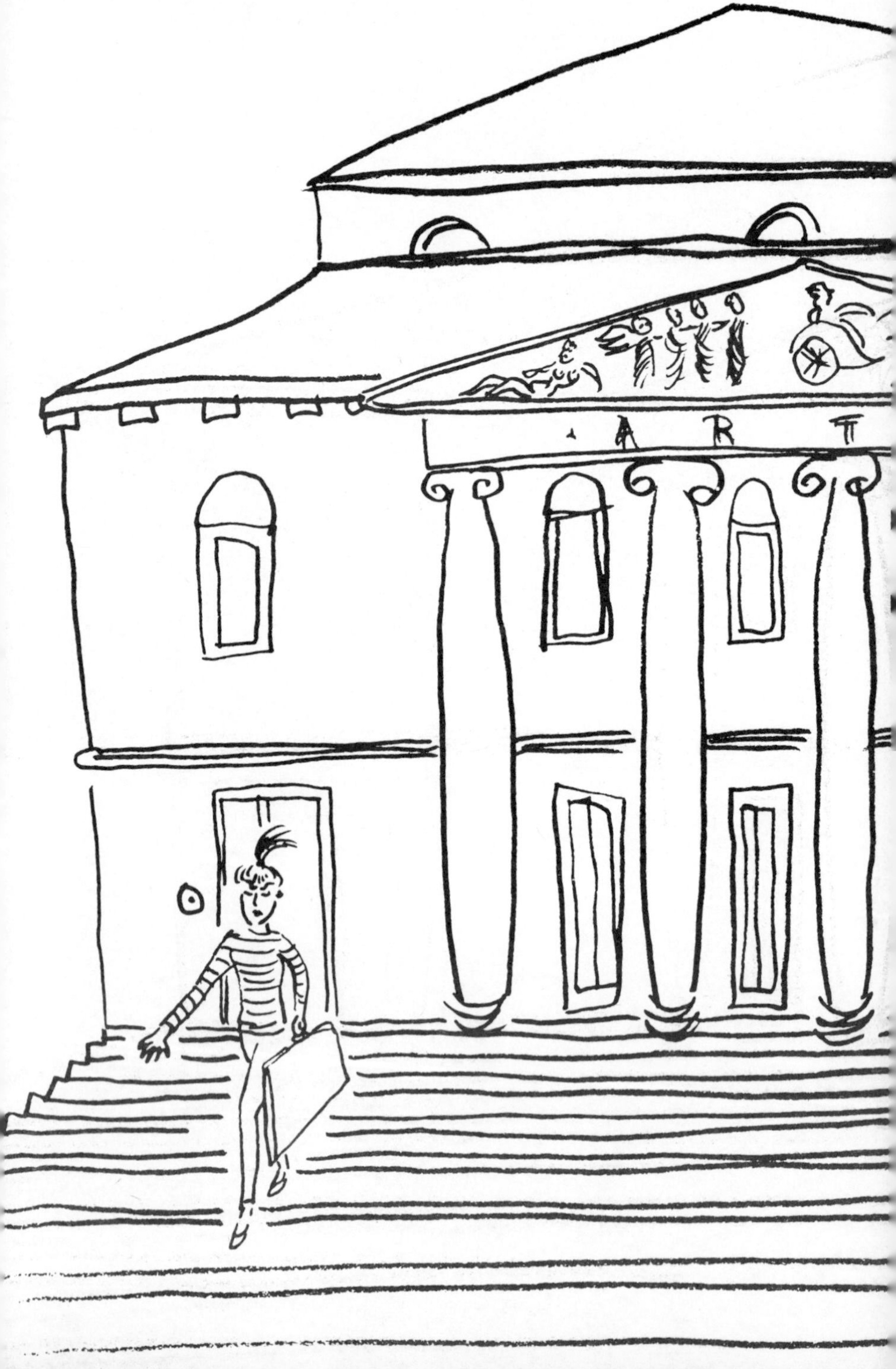
A R T

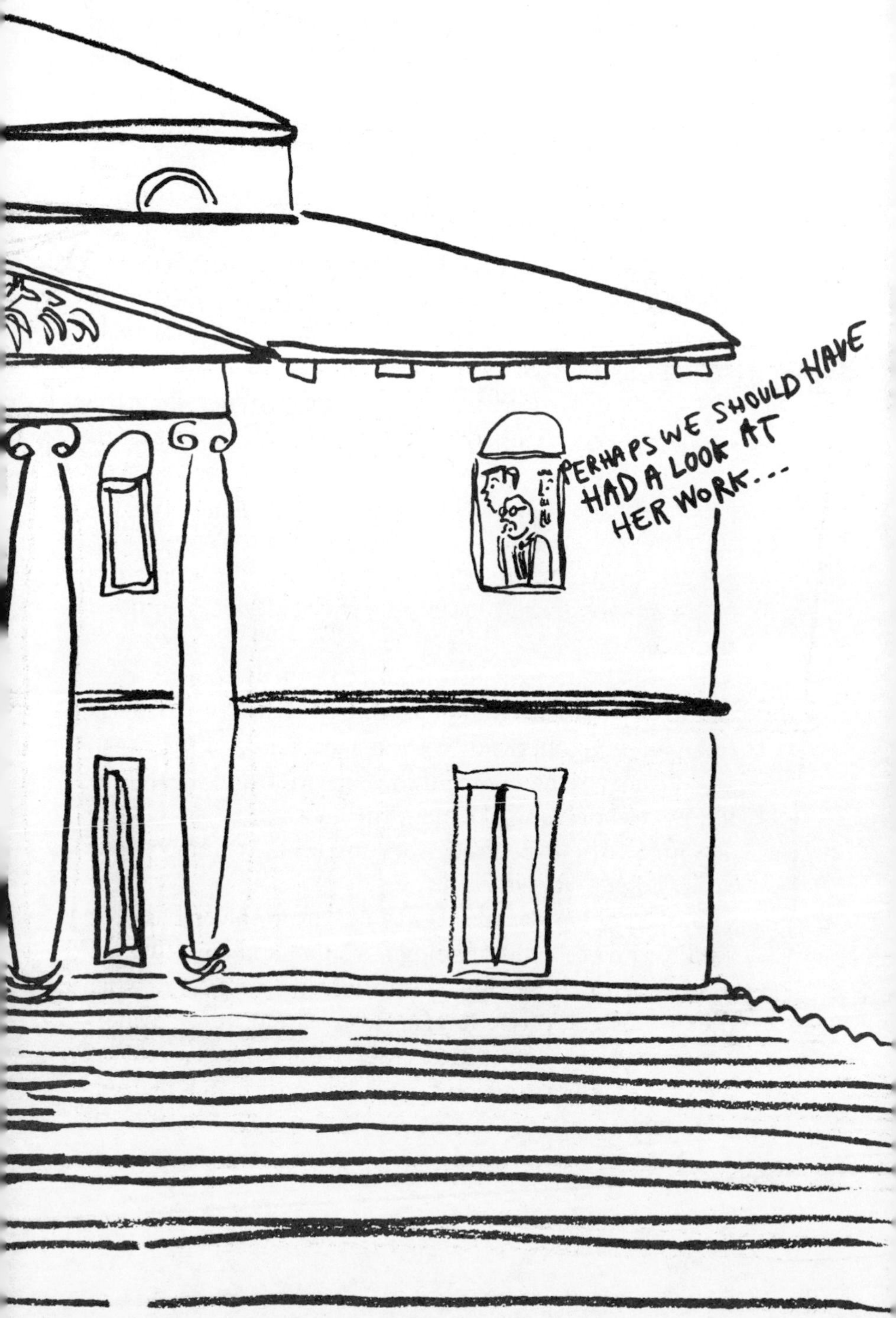
PERHAPS WE SHOULD HAVE HAD A LOOK AT HER WORK...

What all these institutions represent is the professional face of art – the face with all the power. Women are not excluded, of course. No one would dare do that today! But because men fill most of the positions of authority and run most of the institutions, they are in control of who they let in beside them and who they encourage to follow them.

The art establishment is like a gentleman's club. It lets in a few women because the climate of the time demands it, but it has no intention of letting in too many. It would be insane if it did. For the art establishment is a male professional association, with more applicants than places. And what profession ever willingly lessened the chances for its members? Lack of qualifications or experience are the 'reasons' which transform the exclusion of women into the respectable 'protection of professional standards'. Sometimes it seems as if they only let in enough women to protect themselves from the accusation of sexism, or to add variety to the male faces running things.

If women are excluded from most of the power, they cannot act as men do and encourage the work of their sex or argue sympathetically for the acceptance of their own sex. Women remain forever the exception and the minority, instead of being like men, the *norm*. Because they are abnormal, the exception, they are seen as women first, professionals second.

In the last two decades a great deal of attention has been paid to the problems of being a woman and an artist. Far from being depressed into frustration and inaction by what they see, women artists and art historians have been energized. Some of today's most interesting work is produced by artists whose subject matter has grown out of their experience as women. Some of today's most interesting art history is written by women whose research into female artists of the past has thrown fresh light on the societies in which they lived. Often the artists and writers bolster each other up, the historians' research and analyses supplying a history and a context for the artists. For example, an awareness of pitfalls facing women artists in the past has made today's artists aware that strategy plays as important a part in their success as talent.

Some go along with the system, believing that though acceptance by the art establishment is harder for women, it is still the only real proof of success.

Some disapprove so strongly of the system that they remove themselves from it into an alternative network of women's galleries. The advantage is access to new exhibiting spaces and a sympathetic audience; the disadvantage is that it allows the mainstream to regard their work as a fringe effort not worthy of critical attention.

The majority enter the system but refuse to keep quiet about its faults or its prejudices. The lessons of art history have taught them to stand up for themselves and they have been rewarded for doing so. There are more of them around than there were and they are listened to more politely. In enlightened circles it is no longer acceptable to put women down and they have benefited to a small degree from this.

In the past twenty years, feminist art historians have been exposing the way the male bias of art history writes women down or out of art.

When Petersen and Wilson were researching their book *Women Artists*, they found that many women turned up under the names of male artists: 'We discovered that if we looked up the family names of well known male artists we often found some account of a wife/lover/sister/daughter who was an artist, too.'

Traditional art historians have a habit of equating lover, wife or mother with *inferior*. In the *Pelican History*, Suzanne Valadon does not achieve her own personal entry. She is to be found under the entry for Maurice Utrillo:

'His mother, Suzanne Valadon (1867–1938), had been a model for Puvis de Chavannes, Renoir, and Lautrec, and was herself a respectable draughtsman if an indifferent painter.'

It is the same lukewarm praise as is given to Augustus in the same book. Yet John has an entry to himself.

Traditional art historians deny women their due by their assumption that 'real' artists belong to the male sex. When they write about women a tone of amazement creeps in, implying that an untutored natural talent and not a trained artist had surprisingly produced the work.

Hannah Höch has earned her place in twentieth century art as a founder of German Dada. According to the *Pelican History*, the masters of photo montage were Raoul Haussmann and John Heartfield. But we also learn that 'The collages of Hannah Höch, Haussmann's companion during the Dada years, are scarcely inferior to his.' Hannah Höch considered that she and Haussmann developed their work together, as Picasso and Braque had done in the Cubist years. This Picasso-Braque collaboration has never bothered art historians. Yet when one of the workers is a woman – and a 'companion' at that – her input is downgraded, even if only to 'scarcely inferior'. What does 'scarcely inferior' actually mean? Why does the writer have such trouble saying it is *as good as*? Could it be that the artist is a woman?

Traditional art historians have tended to ignore the women members of the movements that have succeeded each other like strata over the past hundred years. There are books galore about the Impressionists, surely the most documented art movement of the last hundred years. But much less discussion is given to the women members of the group.

One excuse is that Eva Gonzalez died young, though one suspects that if she had been a man she would have become a 'tragically unfulfilled genius'.

But Berthe Morisot, whose colouring is subtle and her brush work dazzlingly and daringly loose, has never been given her due. It is impossible to think of a male painter so closely connected with an important art movement whose work has been so little reproduced and analysed.

When in 1962 William Roberts painted a retrospective portrait of the Vorticists, the group of artists he belonged to in London before the outbreak of the first world war, he included two women, Jessica Dismorr and Helen Saunders, in the line-up. Yet the *Pelican History* mentions no women in all the pages it devotes to Vorticism.

A fascinating development of contemporary interest in women and art is the debate over the existence of a recognisably *female* art.

The American artist Judy Chicago is sure there is such a thing. In her autobiography, *Through the Flower*, she claimed that women artists like Barbara Hepworth and Georgia O'Keeffe had used and were still using central imagery – often hidden or disguised – related to their biology. This equation between womb and central composition is not to the taste of all women artists. For one thing, the theory does not apply to them all. And for another many are wary of having their art labelled 'female' by a biological imagery which has traditionally been used as evidence of their inferiority.

The question of whether a woman's hand reveals itself in style or subject matter has never been satisfactorily answered. The pitfalls of claiming a feminine hand is revealed by comparing a picture by Berthe Morisot with one by Monet.

Can *you* tell which is by the man, and which the woman?

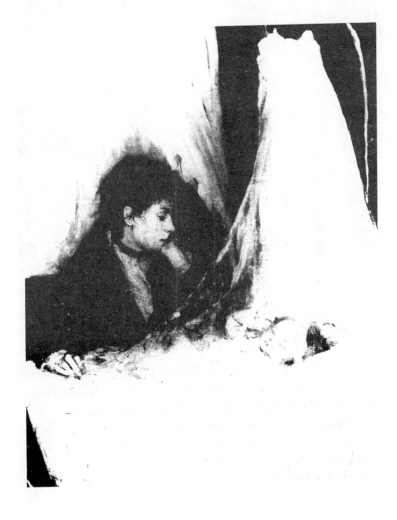

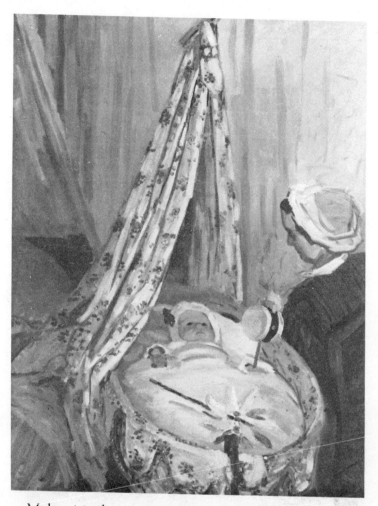

Male critics have automatically believed they could tell – but only, it now appears, when they knew the work was by a woman. Then, and only then, could they point with confidence to the 'feminine' subject matter, or the 'feminine' use of colour. When they did not know the gender of the artist, the paintings were always considered to be the work of a male hand.

On cleaning, this painting was discovered not to be by the famous seventeenth century Dutch painter Franz Hals, as London's National Gallery had previously thought, but by the less famous, but clearly equally good, seventeenth century Dutch painter Judith Leystar.

Artemisia Gentileschi painted this picture of *Judith Decapitating Holofernes*.

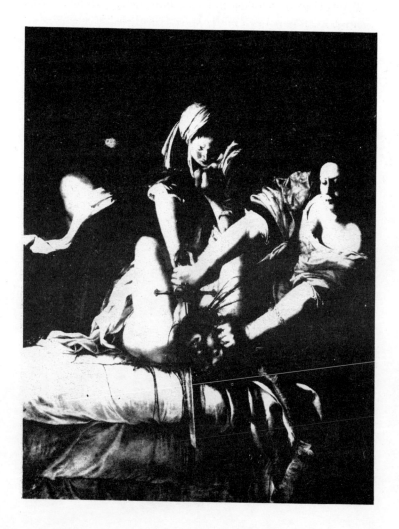

Artemisia had been raped. Does it show in the painting? According to her father, 'She was deflowered by force and known in the flesh many a time by Agostino Tasso, painter, close friend and colleague of the petitioner.' In a Roman court on March 18, 1612, Artemisia testified that the rape occurred when she was alone in the studio with her father's friend. Cross-examined under torture, she stuck to her story: she had wounded her attacker as she fought him. Given this experience there is a strong temptation to read a painting like *Judith Decapitating Holofernes* as her revenge on the rapist. But if the picture is compared with a work by Caravaggio, by whose paintings she was inspired, then it seems to belong as much to her times as to her personal experience.

Linda Nochlin has summed up the debate:

'Many contemporary feminists assert that there is actually a different kind of greatness for women's art than for men's. They propose the existence of a distinctive and recognisable feminine style, differing in both formal and expressive qualities from that of men artists and posited on the unique character of women's situation and experience.

'This might seem reasonable enough: in general, women's experience and situation in society, and hence as artists, differs from men's, and certainly an art produced by a group of consciously united and purposely articulate women intent on bodying forth a group consciousness of feminine experience might indeed be stylistically identifiable as feminist, if not feminine, art. This remains within the realms of possibility; so far it has not occurred.

'No subtle essence of feminity would seem to link the work of Artemisia Gentileschi, Mme Vigée-Lebrun, Angelika Kauffmann, Rosa Bonheur, etc. In every instance women artists and writers would seem to be closer to other artists and writers of their own period and outlook than they are to each other.'

Since 1971, when that was written, the terms of the debate have shifted. While it is accepted that women artists paint in the style of their times and that it is an arid exercise to look for a 'subtle essence of femininity', many art historians today argue that women artists – like their male counterparts – must have painted their view of life into their work. Even though many of Artemisia's female subjects – Bathsheba, Judith and Susanna – were painted by the male artists of the time, she was not forced to choose them. She picked them from a number of available subjects and themes because they meshed with her personal experience of life and of being a woman.

In one area, events have overtaken Linda Nochlin. When she wrote that a 'group consciousness of feminine experience' had not occurred, it was the days before women artists refused to have their way of viewing life rejected. Since the seventies, women artists have been the leaders of one of the most exciting areas of contemporary art: the development of new subject matter.

Themes in art have been remarkably fixed over the past 500 years, but women artists are adding a few of their own, arguing that as their experience of society has been unlike that of men, their work should mirror this.

In the 1970s a group of British women artists started to make art objects small enough to send to each other through the post. 'Art not Heart' was embroidered on a cushion. 'Homemade I'm afraid' was knitted into a panel. Pieces of female anatomy nestled inside chocolate boxes. Cakes were baked in the shape of babies. The resulting collection was exhibited as *Feministo,* to the recognition of women and the discomfort of men not used to seeing themselves and their beliefs put under the artist's eye. Points were being made about the housebound mother's difficulty in making art, and how unadmired domestic crafts were the receptacle for her creativity.

In 1978 Mary Kelly scandalized the newspapers by hanging an exhibition of used nappy liners in a London gallery, an attempt to show her child's development and her reactions to it. The media rationalised their horror by attacking the subject matter as 'not suitable for art'.

In 1982 Susan Hiller photographed her naked pregnant belly month by month. Fascinating, but far from the romantic male view of Maternity with pensive look and hands clasped over tastefully dressed bump.

THREE/ She will bring forth in time. Their "we" will be extended, her "I" will be altered, enlarged or annihilated. This is the terror hidden in bliss − − She keeps on describing bodily states, as though that will help her incorporate the changes within her notion of 'self'.

Men have always felt free to put their feelings about Woman into art and literature. Women are harpies, shrews, beauties, virgins, vindictive mistresses. No one gets up and boos in the opera house when the tenor sings that Woman is fickle or barracks in the theatre when Shakespeare writes that Woman is like a child, or feels anything but Awe In Front of Art when Titian paints Eve as a wily beauty luring an utterly innocent Adam.

But when Elena Samperi painted her feeling about Man in *Madonna* (1980), showing him as a miniature adult in a schoolboy cap endlessly sucking and biting at the breast, there was a deafening outcry about female bitchiness and hatred of men.

This book began politely with a list of women artists. It has developed more pointedly into an attack on the dominance of male views of the world. The shift in these pages from the artists to the society which surrounds them is designed to show that artists do not live in a vacuum where talent and drive are all that is necessary for success. They live in a world of barriers, beliefs and prejudices with which they must learn to cope.

Since it is a world where men make the rules, it is difficult for women to advance into areas where they are not wanted. The cries of outrage aroused by the feminists' art reveal their success in invading territory marked 'Keep Out'.

It is these cries which enable this book to end optimistically. Feminist writings, speeches, analysis, agitation and artwork of the last 15 years have given women the confidence to take themselves seriously as artists and shamed the art establishment into sharing some of its sweets with them. Although still primarily a male affair, art today is far less so than it was. Women artists? Why ever not?

GOING FURTHER

Published in 1928, Virginia Woolf's polemic on the stifling of women's creativity, *A Room of One's Own* (many editions), is still exciting. 'Why Have There Been No Great Women Artists?', Linda Nochlin's essay in *Art and Sexual Politics* (T.B. Hess and E.C. Baker (eds) New York 1973) is a model of how asking the right question can transform knowledge. *The Obstacle Race* by Germaine Greer (1979) is a comprehensive and interesting discussion of hundreds of women artists active up to 1900. *Old Mistresses: Women, Art and Ideology* by Roszika Parker and Griselda Pollock (1981) is an important look at art, artists and art history from a feminist perspective. *Women Artists* by Karen Petersen and J.J. Wilson (New York 1976, London 1985) contains brief accounts of many women artists throughout history and a useful bibliography. *Women's Images of Men*, a collection of essays by women artists and critics edited by Sarah Kent and Jacqueline Morreau (1985), discusses what happens when the traditional male artist/female model roles are reversed.

Exhibition catalogues, biography and autobiography are other important sources. In *Canvassing* (1986), for example, Pamela Gerrish Nunn presents excerpts from the writings of six Victorian women artists.

Most public galleries have works by women, but not always on display. You can always ask to see them and enquire why they are not on permanent display.

For further research into women and art, contact the ever-helpful Women Artists Slide Library, Old Town Hall, Lavendar Hill, London S.W.11.

Other Works Cited in the Text

Kathy Adler and Tamar Garb (eds), *The Correspondence of Berthe Morisot*, 1986.

Wendy Baron, *The Camden Town Group*, 1979.

Judy Chicago, *Through The Flower*, New York 1977.

Susan Chitty, *Gwen John, 1876 – 1939*, 1981.

David Garrett (ed), *Carrington – Letters and Extracts From Her Diaries*.

Artemisia Gentileschi, *Atti di un processo per stupro*, Milan 1981.

George Heard Hamilton, *Painting and Sculpture in Europe, 1880 – 1940*, Harmondsworth 1972.

Hubert Herkomer, *My School and My Gospel*, 1908.

Sidney Hutchison, *The History of The Royal Academy*, 1968.

Dorothy M. Mayer, *Angelica Kauffmann RA*, Gerrards Cross 1972.

John Thomas Smith, *Nollekens and His Times*, 1828.

Elizabeth Vigée-Lebrun, *Souvenirs*, Paris 1983.

(Place of publication London unless otherwise stated)

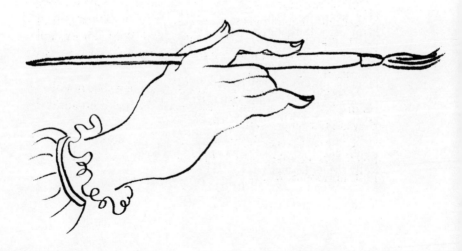

WOMEN ARTISTS
REFERRED TO IN THE TEXT

Anguissola, Sofonisba (Italian), 1530s – 1625
Bell, Vanessa (British), 1879 – 1961
Bonheur, Frances Rosa (French), 1822 – 1899
Carriera, Giovanna (Italian), dates unknown
Carriera, Rosalba (Italian), 1675 – 1757
Carrington, Dora (British), 1893 – 1932
Cassatt, Mary (American), 1844 – 1926
Chicago, Judy (American), 1939 –
Delany, Mary (British), 1700 – 1788
Delauney, Sonia Terk (French), 1885 – 1979
Dismorr, Jessica (British), 1885 – 1939
Fontana, Lavinia (Italian), 1552 – 1614
Gentileschi, Artemisia (Italian), 1593 – 1653
Goncharova, Natalia (Russian), 1881 – 1962
Gonzales, Eva (French), 1849 – 1883
Greenaway, Kate (British), 1846 – 1901
Hemessen, Katherina de (German), 1527 – 1566?
Hepworth, Barbara (British), 1903 – 1975
Herford, Laura (British), 1831 – 1870
Hiller, Susan (American), 1942 –
Höch, Hannah (German), 1889 – 1978
Hosmer, Harriet (American), 1830 – 1908
John, Gwen (British), 1876 – 1939
Jopling, Louise (British), 1843 – 1933
Kauffmann, Angelika (Swiss), 1741 – 1807
Kelly, Mary (American), 1941 –
Kemp-Welch, Lucy (British), 1869 – 1958
Knight, Laura (British), 1877 – 1970

Kollwitz, Käthe (German), 1867 – 1945
Labille-Guiard, Adélaïde (French), 1744 – 1803
Leyster, Judith (Dutch), 1609 – 1660
McNeill, Dorelia (British), 1881 – 1969
Merian, Sybilla (Dutch), 1647 – 1717
Modersohn-Becker, Paula (German), 1876 – 1907
Morisot, Berthe (French), 1841 – 1895
Moser, Mary (British), 1744 – 1819
Nelli, Plautilla (Italian), sixteenth century
Nettleship, Ida (British), 1877 – 1907
O'Keeffe, Georgia (American), 1887 –
Rae, Henrietta (British), 1859 – 1928
Riley, Bridget (British), 1931 –
Ruysch, Rachel (Dutch), 1664 – 1750
Samperi, Elena (Italian), 1951 –
Saunders, Helen (British), 1885 – 1963
Steinbach, Sabina von (German), fourteenth century
Swynnerton, Annie (British), 1844 – 1933
Thompson, Elizabeth (Lady Butler) (British), 1844 – 1933
Valadon, Suzanne (French), 1865 – 1938
Vigée-Lebrun, Elizabeth (French), 1755 – 1842

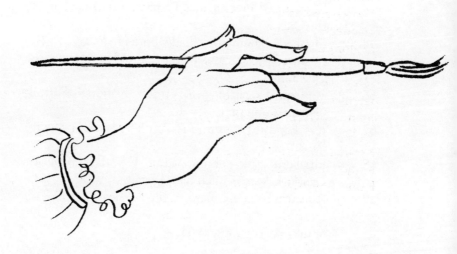

WORKS REPRODUCED